Easy Learning

Telling the time practice

Age 5-7

My name is _____.

I am _____ years old.

I go to _____ School.

My birthday is _____.

Happy Birthday

Ian Jacques

How to use this book

- Find a quiet, comfortable place to work, away from other distractions.

- Tackle one topic at a time.

- Help with reading the instructions where necessary, and ensure that your child understands what to do.

- Discuss with your child what they have learnt.

- Let your child return to their favourite pages once they have been completed, to talk about the activities.

- Reward your child with plenty of praise and encouragement.

Special features

- Yellow boxes: Introduce and outline the key ideas in each section.

- Yellow shaded boxes: Offer advice to parents on how to consolidate your child's understanding.

- Games: There are two games provided at the end of the book which reinforce the whole topic.

Published by Collins
An imprint of HarperCollins*Publishers*
77–85 Fulham Palace Road
Hammersmith
London
W6 8JB

Browse the complete Collins catalogue at www.collins.co.uk

© HarperCollins*Publishers* 2011

10 9 8 7 6 5 4 3 2

ISBN-13 978-0-00-746162-2

MIX
Paper from
responsible sources
FSC™ C007454

FSC™ is a non-profit international organisation established to promote the responsible management of the world's forests. Products carrying the FSC label are independently certified to assure consumers that they come from forests that are managed to meet the social, economic and ecological needs of present and future generations, and other controlled sources.

Find out more about HarperCollins and the environment at
www.harpercollins.co.uk/green

The authors assert their moral rights to be identified as the authors of this work.

British Library Cataloguing in Publication Data

A Catalogue record for this publication is available from the British Library

Written by Ian Jacques
Composition by Linda Miles, Lodestone Publishing Ltd
Illustrated by Graham Smith
Cover design by Linda Miles, Lodestone Publishing Ltd
Cover illustration by Kathy Baxendale
Project managed by Chantal Peacock
Printed in China

Contents

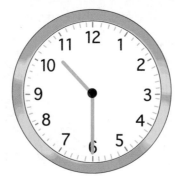

How to use this book	2
Day and night	4
Months and seasons	6
Days of the week	8
Time words	10
On the hour times	12
Half past times	14
Practice questions	16
Putting hands on the clock	18
Quarter past times	20
Quarter to times	22
Practice questions	24
Race game	28
Pairs game	30
Answers	32

The day begins with sunrise when it gets light outside.

The night begins with sunset when it gets dark outside.

Q1 Look at the two pictures above. Find four differences between them.

1 _____

_____

2 _____

_____

3 _____

_____

4 _____

_____

Talk about the differences in these particular pictures and then extend the conversation to include differences in other familiar situations.

Q2 Write the words **morning**, **afternoon** or **evening** in the spaces.

I go to bed in the _____

I eat my breakfast in the _____

I come home from school in the _____

I brush my teeth in the _____ and _____

The sun sets in the _____

My last birthday party took place in the _____

Q3 Draw a picture to show something that you do in the morning and something different that you do in the evening.

Morning	Evening

For most children, morning is the period between getting up and lunchtime, afternoon is the period between lunch and dinner, and evening takes them through to bedtime.

There are 12 months in a year.
The year begins in January.

Winter

Autumn

December
January
November
February
October
March
September
April
August
May
July
June

Spring

Summer

Q1 Write down the month which is just before

April _____

September _____

January _____

Q2 Write down the month which is just after

October _____

June _____

February _____

It is worth pausing here and learning the ordering of the months and their correct spelling.

Q3 Write the season under each picture.

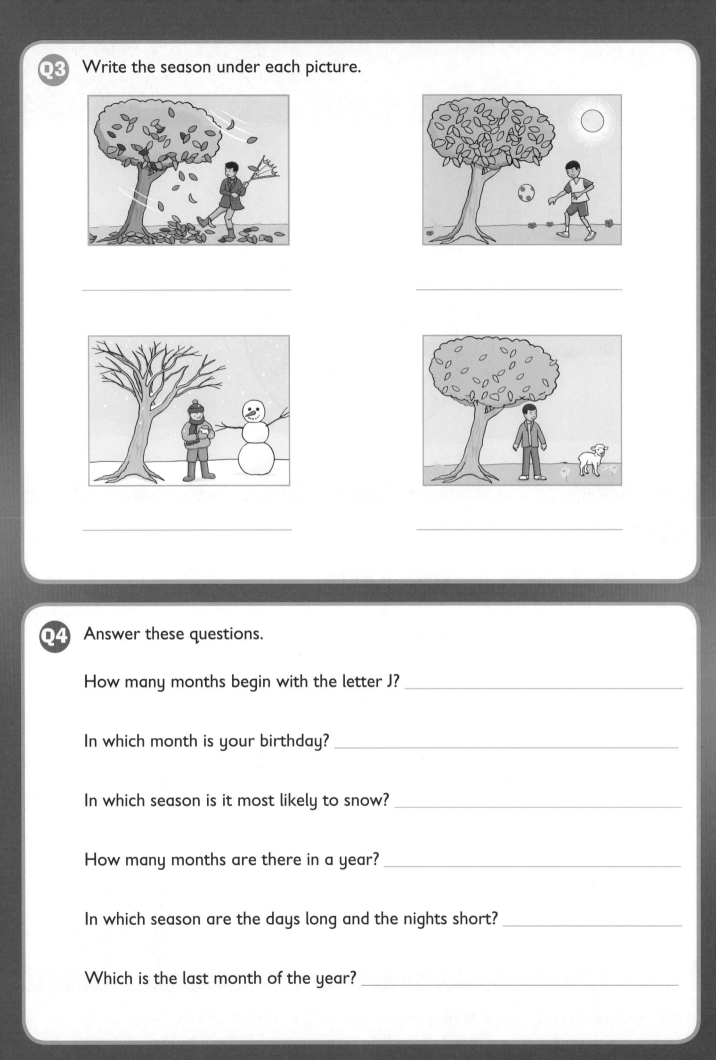

_____   _____

_____   _____

Q4 Answer these questions.

How many months begin with the letter J? _____

In which month is your birthday? _____

In which season is it most likely to snow? _____

How many months are there in a year? _____

In which season are the days long and the nights short? _____

Which is the last month of the year? _____

Days of the week

There are 7 days in a week.

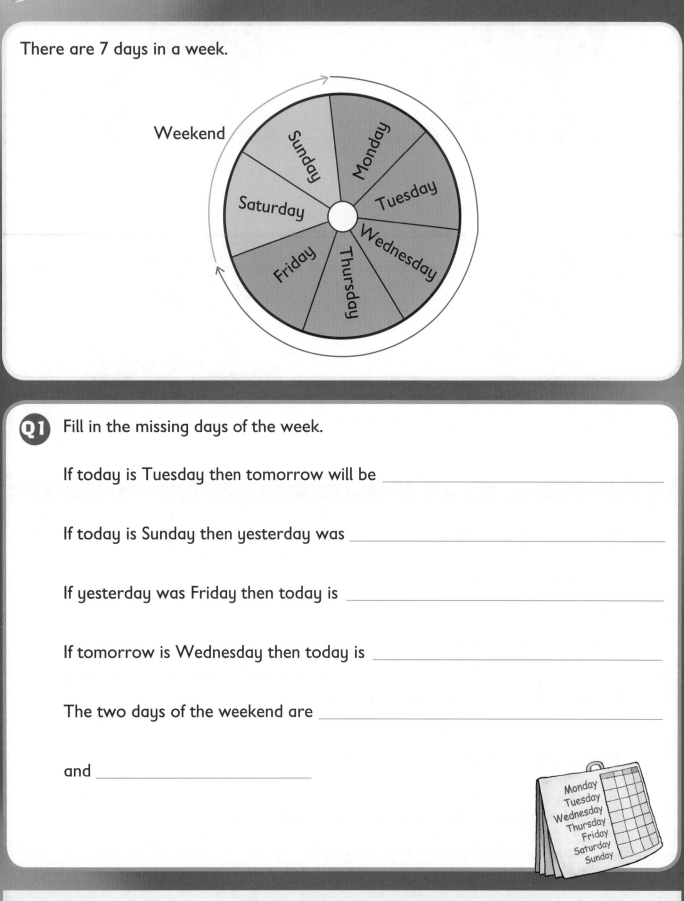

Q1 Fill in the missing days of the week.

If today is Tuesday then tomorrow will be _____

If today is Sunday then yesterday was _____

If yesterday was Friday then today is _____

If tomorrow is Wednesday then today is _____

The two days of the weekend are _____

and _____

It is worth learning the order of the days of the week and their correct spelling.

Q2 Write down the name of your favourite TV programme and a fun activity that you do each day next week.

Day	TV Programme	Activity
Monday		
Tuesday		
Wednesday		
Thursday		
Friday		
Saturday		
Sunday		

Q3 The letters in these words have been muddled up.
Put the letters in the correct order to spell the days of the week.

AYEUSDT _____

USYNDA _____

DEAENSWYD _____

TSUAYADR _____

DIYARF _____

ADMNOY _____

SDYAHRUT _____

A **second** is a very short time. It takes a second to clap your hands.

There are 60 seconds in a **minute**. You can eat a chewy sweet in a minute.

There are 60 minutes in an **hour**. An hour is quite a long time.
Your lunch break at school is about an hour.

Q1 Would you use **seconds**, **minutes** or **hours** to time these activities?

To eat your breakfast in the morning _____

To sneeze _____

Time spent at school each day _____

To get to school in the morning _____

To run across the park _____

Time spent sleeping each day _____

To say 'hello' to someone _____

Time spent at a friend's party _____

Try asking your child to close their eyes and open them again after one minute. Time them to see how good they are at estimating a minute. You can make this into a fun game.

Q2 How many times can you do each of these activities in a **minute?**

Jump up and down on the spot _____

Write your name _____

Put one sock on and off again _____

Count up to ten _____

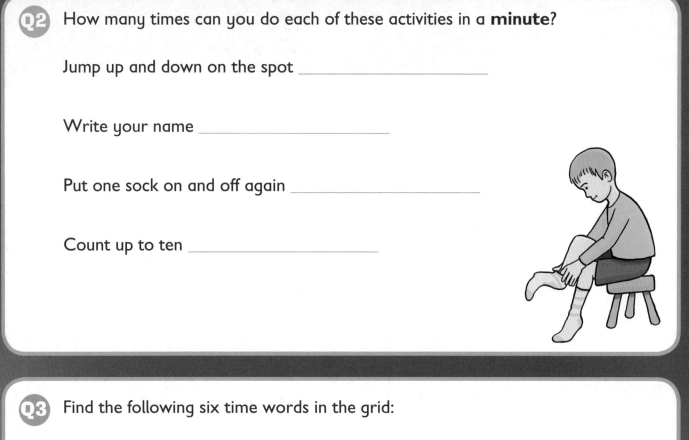

Q3 Find the following six time words in the grid:

second   hour   day   year   summer   week

B	W	F	Z	L	G
S	E	C	O	N	D
Q	E	H	D	A	Y
Y	K	X	O	T	E
J	G	P	V	U	A
S	U	M	M	E	R

Do these activities with your child. In **Q2**, time and count for them as they do the activities.
In **Q3**, the words can be given vertically, horizontally or diagonally. The one on the diagonal is the hardest to spot.

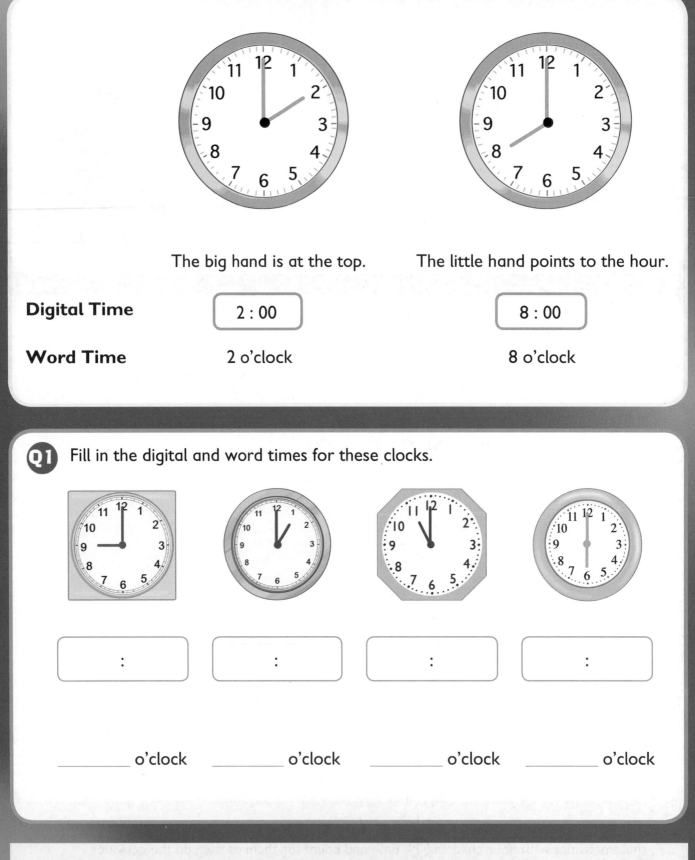

The big hand is at the top.

The little hand points to the hour.

Digital Time

2 : 00

8 : 00

Word Time

2 o'clock

8 o'clock

Q1 Fill in the digital and word times for these clocks.

:

:

:

:

_____ o'clock   _____ o'clock   _____ o'clock   _____ o'clock

Use a real clock or watch at home and make the times relevant to your child by showing the time on the clock when they go to bed, leave the house to go to school and so on.

Q2 Fill in the missing word times.

4 : 00

_____ o'clock

12 : 00

_____ o'clock

5 : 00

_____ o'clock

6 : 00

_____ o'clock

Q3 Fill in the missing digital times.

| : | : | : | : |

2 o'clock   10 o'clock   7 o'clock   3 o'clock

Q4 Put these in time order and then use the letters under each clock to spell a mystery word. Start with the earliest time.

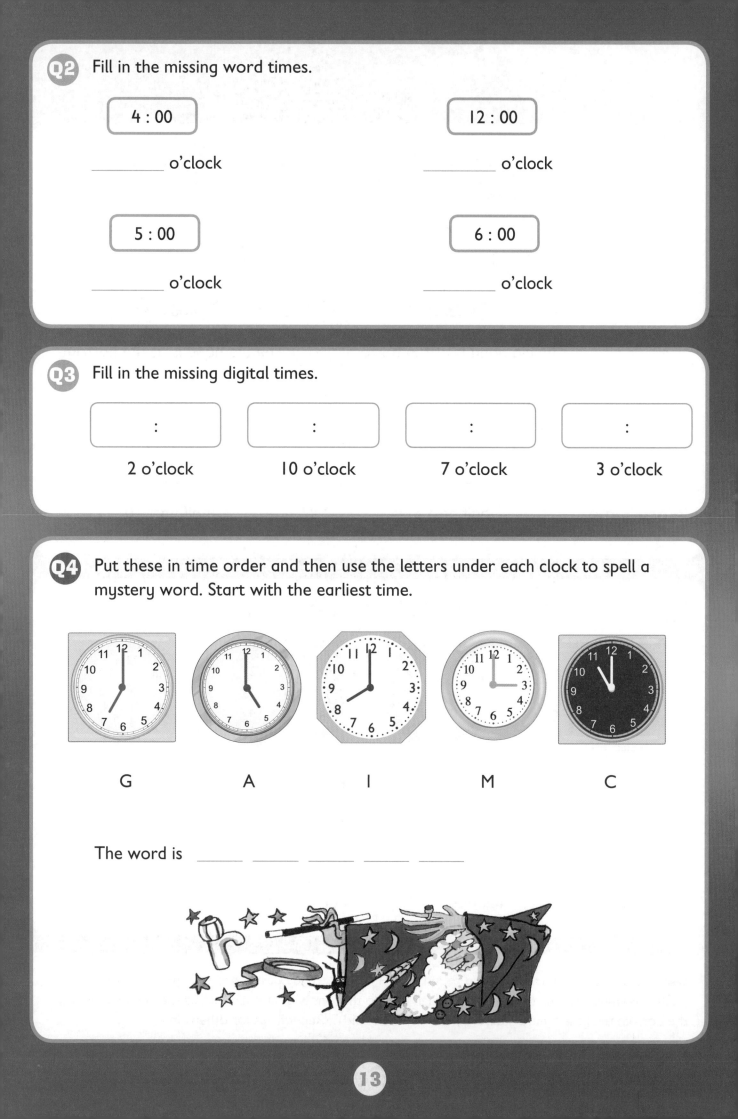

G   A   I   M   C

The word is _____ _____ _____ _____ _____

Half past times

The big hand is at the bottom. The little hand is halfway between 3 and 4.

The big hand is at the bottom. The little hand is halfway between 10 and 11.

Digital Time

| 3 : 30 | 10 : 30 |

Word Time   half past 3   half past 10

Q1 Fill in the digital and word times for these clocks.

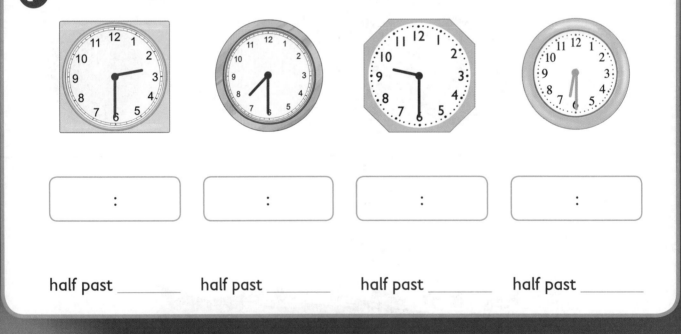

| : | : | : | : |

half past _____   half past _____   half past _____   half past _____

Use a real clock and move the hand round from 4 o'clock to half past 4 and then on to 5 o'clock. Point out what happens to both hands when you do this. Show your child that as the big hand passes the bottom the little hand is halfway between the 4 and 5. Repeat this for other times.

Q2 Fill in the missing word times.

12 : 30

half past _____

1 : 30

half past _____

4 : 30

half past _____

8 : 30

half past _____

Q3 Fill in the missing digital times.

:		:		:		:

half past 9   half past 3   half past 11   half past 5

Q4 What time will it be one hour later than

9 : 30		:
6 : 30		:
2 : 30		:
7 : 30		:
12 : 30		:

If your child is confident using the 5 times table, count round the clock face in 5s to explain why half past times are 30 minutes past the hour.

Q1 Write down the missing digital and word times for these clocks.

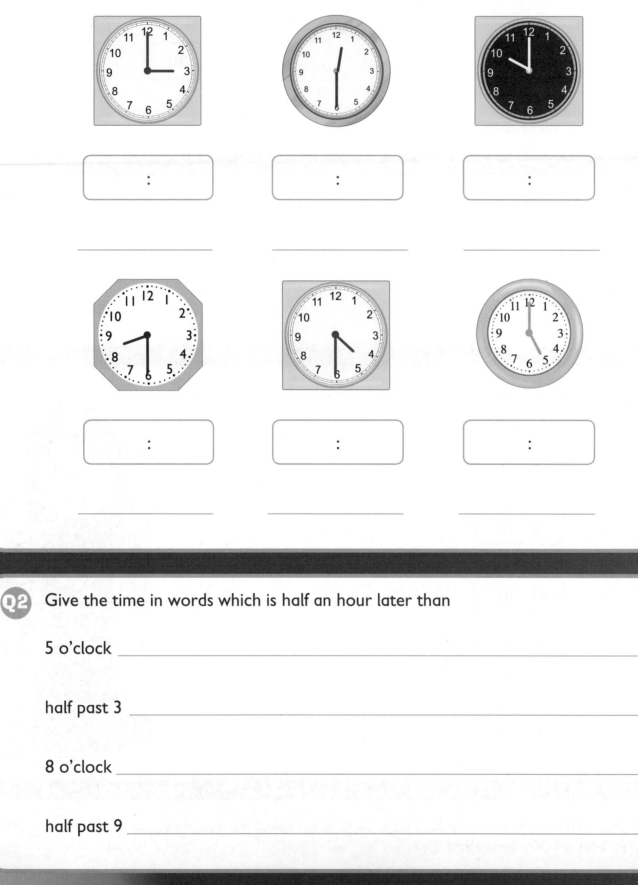

Q2 Give the time in words which is half an hour later than

5 o'clock _____

half past 3 _____

8 o'clock _____

half past 9 _____

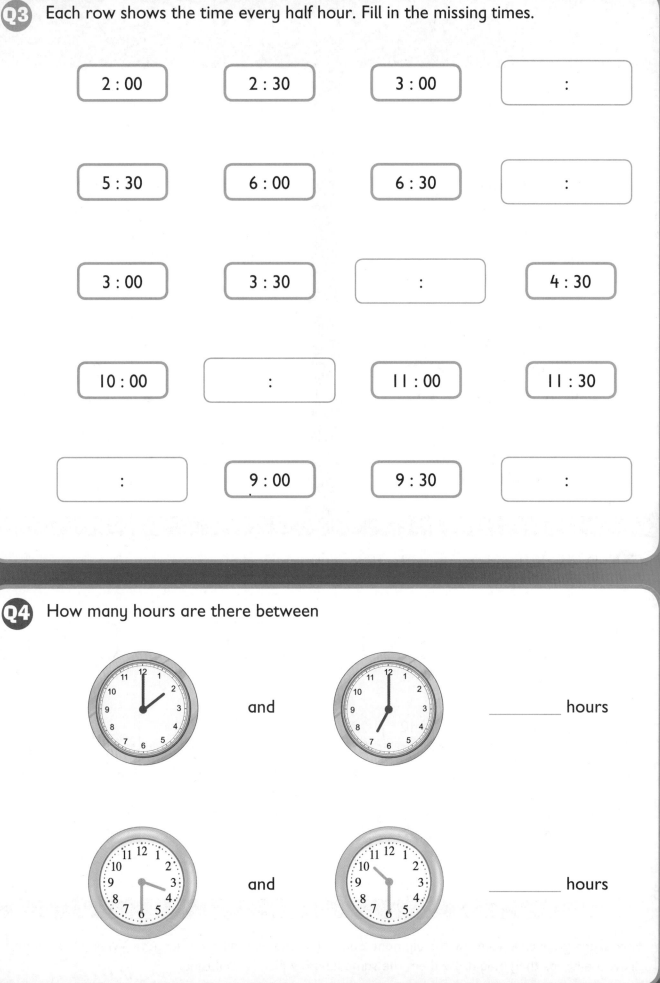

Q3 Each row shows the time every half hour. Fill in the missing times.

| 2 : 00 | 2 : 30 | 3 : 00 | : |

| 5 : 30 | 6 : 00 | 6 : 30 | : |

| 3 : 00 | 3 : 30 | : | 4 : 30 |

| 10 : 00 | : | 11 : 00 | 11 : 30 |

| : | 9 : 00 | 9 : 30 | : |

Q4 How many hours are there between

and   _____ hours

and   _____ hours

17

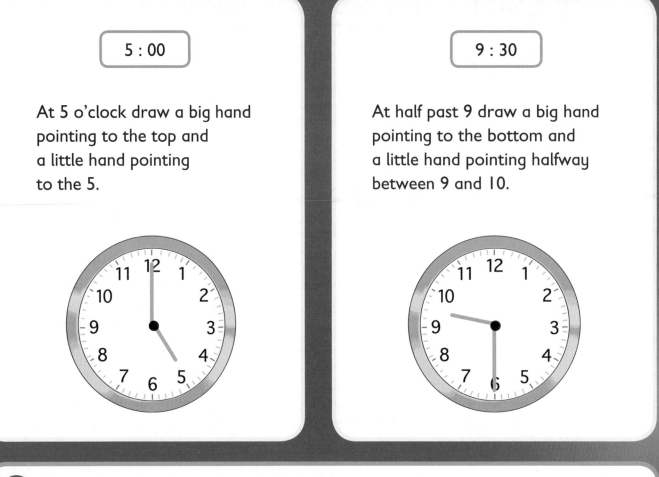

5 : 00

At 5 o'clock draw a big hand pointing to the top and a little hand pointing to the 5.

9 : 30

At half past 9 draw a big hand pointing to the bottom and a little hand pointing halfway between 9 and 10.

Q1 Draw the hands to show the time on these clocks.

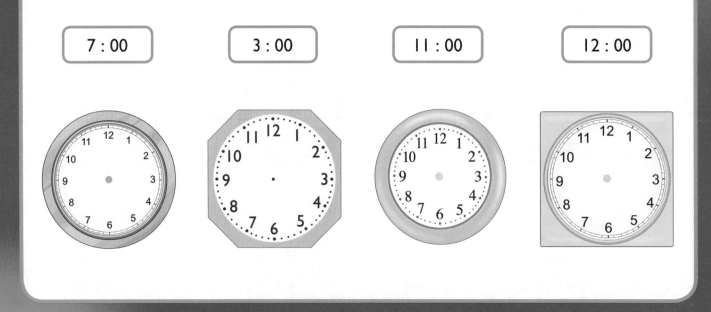

7 : 00

3 : 00

11 : 00

12 : 00

Encourage your child to draw the big hand and little hand with different lengths. When children first draw the hands they may draw them the same length which is confusing.

Q2 Draw the hands to show the time on these clocks.

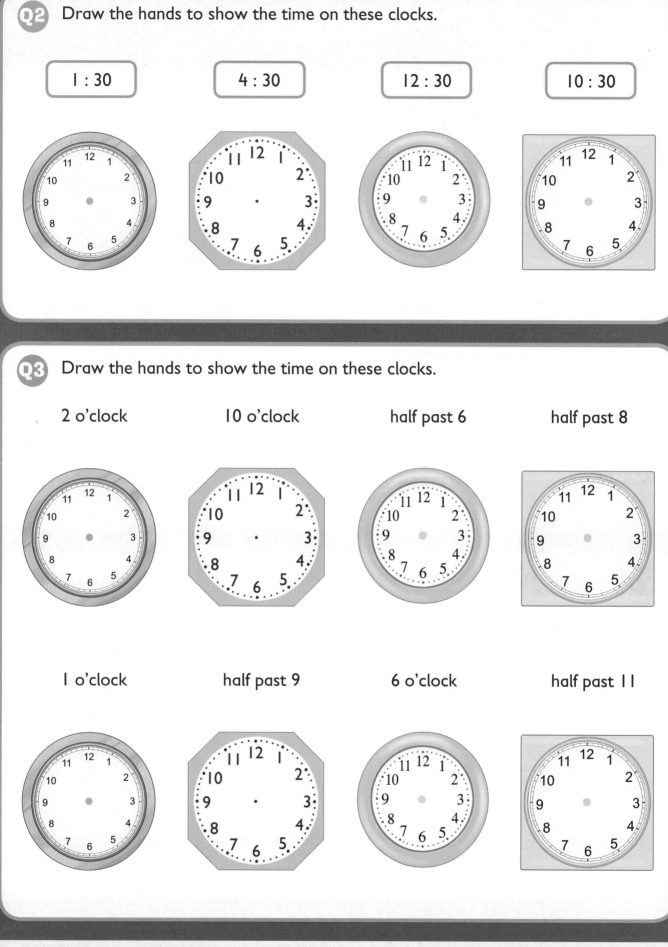

| 1 : 30 | 4 : 30 | 12 : 30 | 10 : 30 |

Q3 Draw the hands to show the time on these clocks.

| 2 o'clock | 10 o'clock | half past 6 | half past 8 |

| 1 o'clock | half past 9 | 6 o'clock | half past 11 |

When drawing the half past times check that the little hand has been drawn in the correct position.

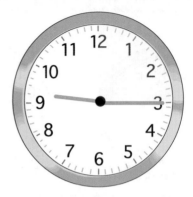

The big hand points to the right. The little hand is just past the 5 on its way to the 6.

The big hand points to the right. The little hand is just past the 9 on its way to the 10.

Digital Time

5 : 15

9 : 15

Word Time

quarter past 5

quarter past 9

Q1 Fill in the digital and word times for these clocks.

| : | : | : | : |

quarter past _____   quarter past _____   quarter past _____   quarter past _____

Move the hands of a real clock from 5 o'clock to quarter past 5 and notice that the little hand has moved towards the 6 but only by a small amount.

Q2 Fill in the missing word times.

4 : 15

quarter past _____

1 : 15

quarter past _____

7 : 15

quarter past _____

10 : 15

quarter past _____

Q3 Fill in the missing digital times.

| : | | : | | : | | : |

quarter past 12   quarter past 2   quarter past 6   quarter past 1

Q4 The rabbit wants to hop home to its burrow through the cabbage patch.
Find a path by colouring in all of the cabbages which show quarter past times.

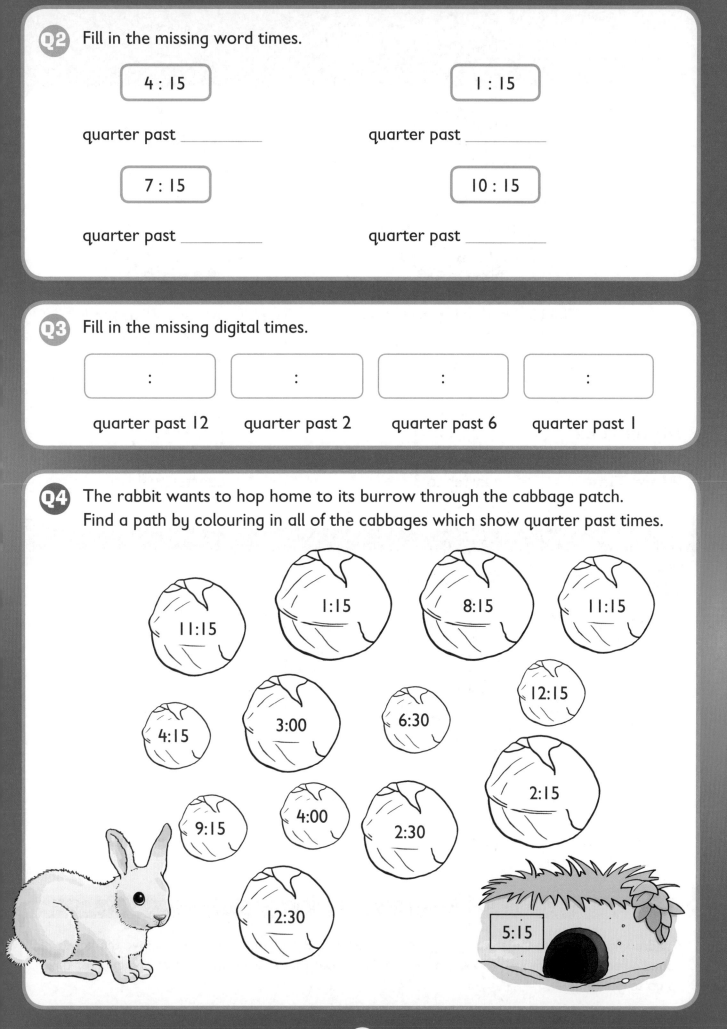

11:15   1:15   8:15   11:15

12:15

4:15   3:00   6:30

2:15

9:15   4:00   2:30

12:30

5:15

21

Quarter to times

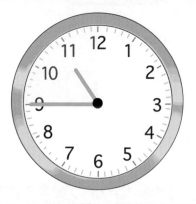

The big hand points to the left.
The little hand is past the 2
and is nearly at the 3.

The big hand points to the left.
The little hand is past the 10
and is nearly at the 11.

Digital Time

2 : 45

10 : 45

Word Time

quarter to 3

quarter to 11

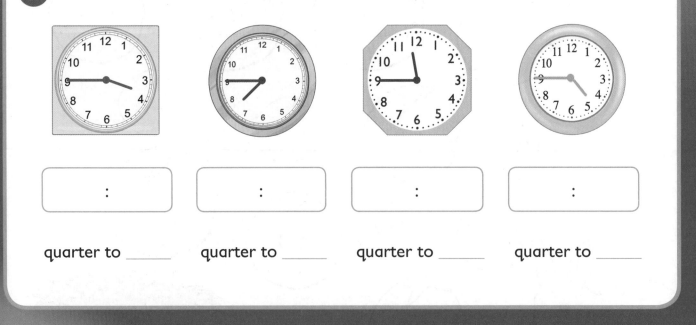

Q1 Fill in the digital and word times for these clocks.

| : | : | : | : |

quarter to _____

quarter to _____

quarter to _____

quarter to _____

Children find it hard to understand why 2:45 is quarter to 3 and not quarter to 2. Move the hands round a real clock from 2:30 to 2:45 to 3:00 and point out that at 2:45 there is just one quarter turn to go to get to 3:00.

Q2 Fill in the missing word times.

| 8 : 45 | | 1 : 45 |

quarter to _____   quarter to _____

| 5 : 45 | | 11 : 45 |

quarter to _____   quarter to _____

Q3 Fill in the missing digital times.

| : | | : | | : | | : |

quarter to 7   quarter to 3   quarter to 9   quarter to 1

Q4 Fill in the missing numbers in this time machine. The first one has been done for you.

4 : 15 →

7 : 45 →

2 : 45 →

5 : 15 →

9 : 45 →

half an hour later

→ 4 : 45

→ :

→ :

→ :

→ :

Q1 Fill in the missing digital times

:   :   :   :

:   :   :   :

Q2 Colour in the following picture. If the time is on the hour colour it **brown**. If the time is half past use **red**, if the time is quarter past use **black**, and if the time is quarter to use **blue**.

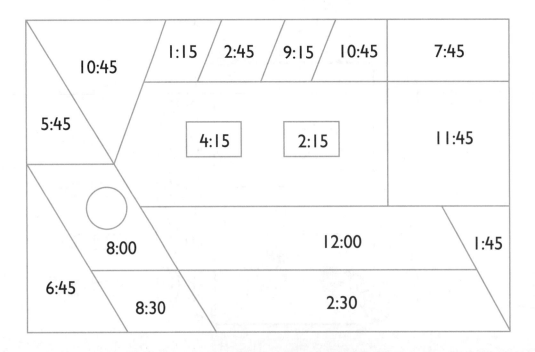

Write down these times in words.

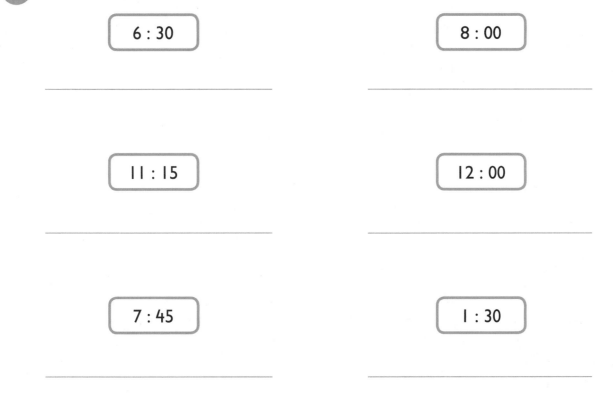

6 : 30

8 : 00

_____

_____

11 : 15

12 : 00

_____

_____

7 : 45

1 : 30

_____

_____

Q4 Join the dots in time order. Start at 3 o'clock and finish at a quarter to 8.
What do you see?

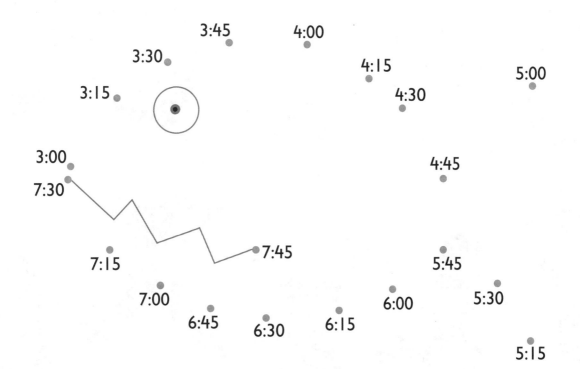

3:45   4:00

3:30

4:15   5:00

3:15   4:30

3:00   4:45

7:30

7:15   7:45

7:00   5:45

6:45   6:30   6:15   6:00   5:30

5:15

Q5 Draw the minute hands on the clocks to show the correct times.

9:00 10:30 3:15 1:45

12:30 7:45 5:00 11:15

Q6 Draw a string to match each child with their balloon.

4:45 12:00 2:15 9:30 3:30

Q7 Fill in the missing digital times.

8 o'clock

[:]

half past 2

[:]

quarter to 4

[:]

quarter past 6

[:]

1 o'clock

[:]

half past 11

[:]

Q8 Answer these questions using digital times.

If it is now 2:30 what time will it be in 3 hours? [:]

What time is half an hour before 8:30? [:]

What is the time 2 hours after 5:15? [:]

What time is a quarter of an hour before 11:15? [:]

What is the time half an hour after 9:00? [:]

If it is 5:45 what time will it be in 1 hour? [:]

What time is 4 hours later than 5:00? [:]

What time is 5 hours earlier than 10:30? [:]

If it is now 7:15 what time will it be in half an hour? [:]

What time is a quarter of an hour after 1:15? [:]

Race game

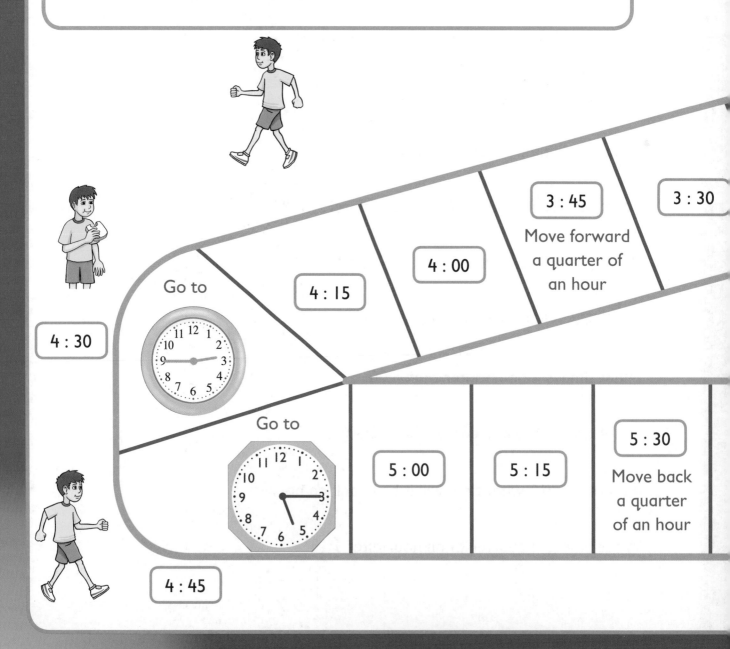

4 : 30

Go to

4 : 15

4 : 00

3 : 45
Move forward a quarter of an hour

3 : 30

Go to

4 : 45

5 : 00

5 : 15

5 : 30
Move back a quarter of an hour

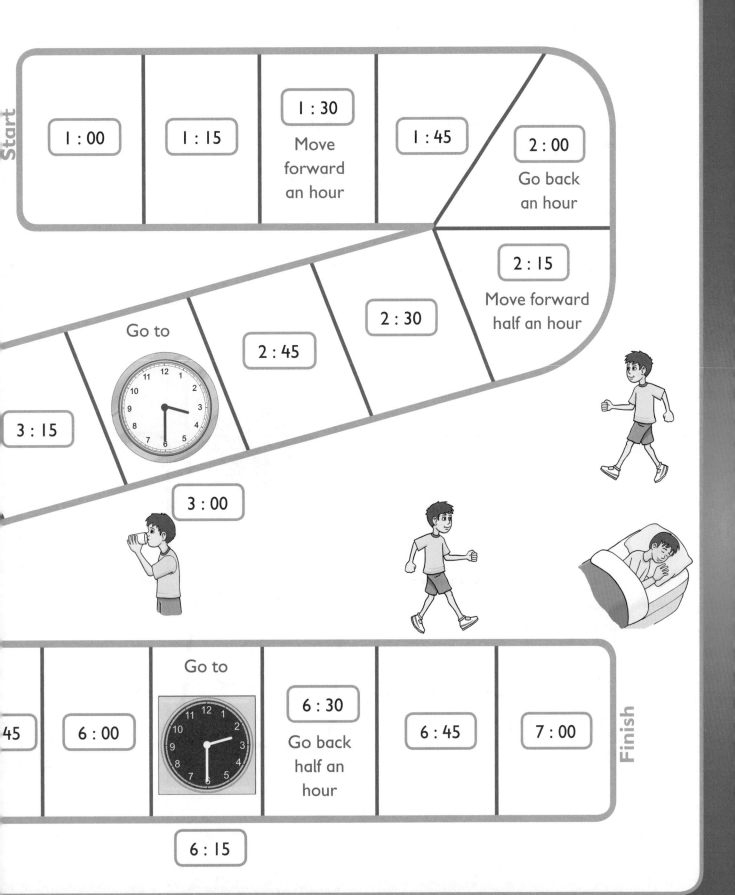

You need: either counters to cover up the squares or copy the cards, cut them out and place them face down on a table or floor.

Rules:

- Take turns at choosing a pair of cards either by moving the counters off the cards or by turning them over.

- If the cards are a matching pair then you win them.

- If not turn them back over (or cover with counters) and the next person picks a pair.

- The person with the most pairs at the end wins.

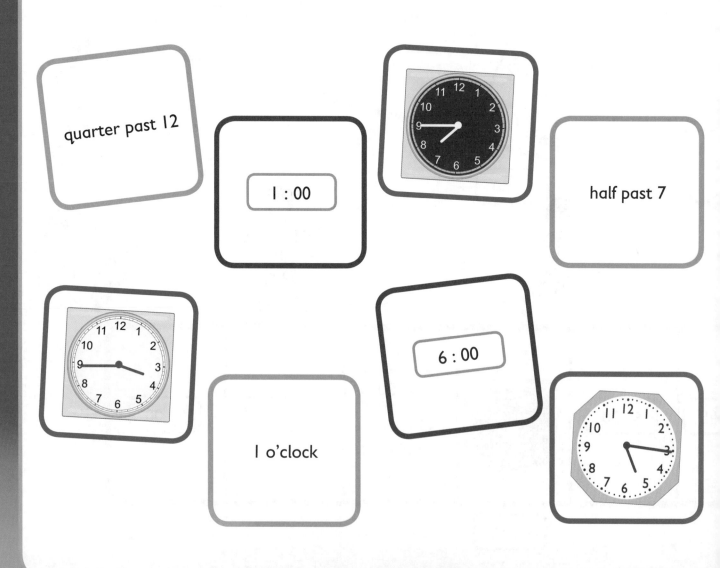

quarter past 12

1 : 00

half past 7

6 : 00

1 o'clock

6 o'clock

2 : 30

half past 2

quarter past 5

7 : 30

4 : 15

quarter to 8

8 : 15

quarter to 4

4 : 45

11 : 45

Answers

Night and day

Page 4

1. 1 In the day the sky is blue and the sun is shining, whereas in the night the sky is black, and there are stars and a moon.
   2 In the day there is a pigeon in the tree whereas at night an owl is near the tree.
   3 In the day children are in the playground whereas at night there are no children, only a fox.
   4 In the day the lamp is off whereas at night the lamp is on.

Page 5

2. evening, morning, afternoon, morning and evening, evening, answers will vary

Months and seasons

Page 6

1. March, August, December
2. November, July, March

Page 7

3. Autumn, Summer
   Winter, Spring
4. 3, answers will vary, Winter, 12, Summer, December

Days of the week

Page 8

1. Wednesday, Saturday, Saturday, Tuesday, Saturday and Sunday

Page 9

2. Answers will vary
3. TUESDAY, SUNDAY, WEDNESDAY, SATURDAY, FRIDAY, MONDAY, THURSDAY

Time words

Page 10

1. minutes, seconds, hours, minutes, seconds, hours, seconds, hours

Page 11

2. Answers will vary
3.

B	W	F	Z	L	G
S	E	C	O	N	D
Q	E	H	D	A	Y
Y	K	X	O	T	E
J	G	P	V	U	A
S	U	M	M	E	R

On the hour times

Page 12

1. 9:00   1:00   11:00   6:00
   9 o'clock 1 o'clock 11 o'clock 6 o'clock

Page 13

2. 4 o'clock, 12 o'clock, 5 o'clock, 6 o'clock
3. 2:00, 10:00, 7:00, 3:00
4. MAGIC

Half past times

Page 14

1. 2:30,   7:30,   9:30,   6:30
   half past 2, half past 7, half past 9, half past 6

Page 15

2. half past 12, half past 1, half past 4, half past 8
3. 9:30, 3:30, 11:30, 5:30
4. 10:30, 7:30, 3:30, 8:30, 1:30

Practice questions

Page 16

1. 3:00   12:30   10:00
   3 o'clock half past 12 10 o'clock
   8:30   4:30   5:00
   half past 8 half past 4 5 o'clock
2. half past 5, 4 o'clock, half past 8, 10 o'clock

Page 17

3. 3:30, 7:00, 4:00, 10:30, 8:30, 10:00
4. 5 hours, 7 hours

Putting hands on the clock

Page 18

1.

Page 19

2.